The Rise and Fall of the Barings at Membland Hall

Arthur L. Clamp

Edward Charles Baring
Born 1828, died 1897. He married Loiusa Bulteel in 1861
having ten children. He was created 1st Lord Revelstoke in 1885 and
was a senior partner in Baring's Bank, London, and a director of the
Bank of England. He purchased Membland house and estate
and lavished a fortune on it but faced financial ruin in 1891
incurring loan debts of £21,000000 in South American investments.

This version of the book is virtually as originally published.
There are now additional pages at the back providing information about the author.

The republishing project is being managed by Arthur's grandson, Steven Gibson. We aim to find all the research that he was involved in publishing, preserving it for the next generation as part of 'The Clamp Collection'.

INTRODUCTION

This booklet records the days of the merchant banking family, the Barings, when they lived in Membland Hall, a mansion on an estate of about 4,135 acres, a mile or so east of Noss Mayo in south-west Devon. It is like a fairy tale story of a very rich London banking merchant marrying a daughter of a nearby gentry family, buying the hall and large estate and lavishing a fortune on them. For a brief period of time it was probably the richest investment in a Devon house which suddenly came to an end in the financial crash of 1890-91 when liabilities of £21 million were incurred in South American enterprises.

Readers may remember the crash in 1995 when a rogue trader on the staff of Barings Bank, London, working in Singapore, lost over £500 million on the Singapore derivatives market bringing to this long established bank another and more serious crisis.

The lineage of the Barings goes back to 1717 when a John Baring was appointed an agent from Germany to supervise the family trade in the woollen industry between Exeter and Bremen. He married a local girl in 1729 with a dowry of £20,000, the start of a massive fortune accumulated through merchant banking over the next 200 years.

The woollen business was transferred to London which later branched out into other commodities then on to banking at an international level. Subsequent sons, grandsons and great grandsons followed increasing the fortune and reputation of Baring Brothers Bank as being of the highest repute and trustworthiness in trading. They were heavily involved in the East India Company buying tea from planters, shipping it to London, and selling it to the merchants.

Another successful venture was investing in the American railroads and the Canadian Pacific Railway Co. The point in Canada where the lines meet is called *Revelstoke* named after the 1st Lord Revelstoke. Between 1865 and 1870 Barings held 28% of American railroad stocks valued at £3,468 million. The funds of the Russian Imperial treasury were held in Baring Brothers Bank, London, standing at £5.4 million. Royalty and others of high standing in this country placed their funds in this bank which was on par with the Rothschild bank. In 1818 the French prime minister said of Barings *that is was the sixth great power in Europe.*

It was into this family that Edward Charles Baring was born in 1828, marrying Louisa Emily Charlotte Bulteel of Pamflete, Holbeton, in 1861 from which ten children were born. The stage was set for the purchase and transformation of Membland Hall and its surrounding buildings and estate as a country mansion for his large family and many visiting dignitaries and friends in the 1880s.

Throughout the 1880s many of the existing buildings were erected, Membland Hall was lavishly furnished, extensive gardens were laid out and, for that period, many modern facilities were installed including a gas supply, telegraph office, covered tennis courts, etc. The full list is given in the sale catalogue of 1915 in this booklet. It makes fascinating reading and gives an good indication of the fortune spent on Membland.

Edward Baring was created the 1st Lord Revelstoke in 1885 heralding a few years of high standing in his society. Membland was at its peak in 1887 when two of Edward Baring's daughters were married. Many famous people came here during the shooting season including the future King Edward VII, Isambard Brunel, Sir Charles Halle, Baron Rothschild, Neville Chamberlain, Gladstone and many others to enjoy the sumptuous hospitality offered by Lord and Lady Revelstoke. This Devonshire retreat was in full splendour during the annual shooting season and at Christmas when the family came together with many friends to hold a large annual party in the covered tennis courts and perform a play in French. Edward Baring spent most of his time at his equally sumptuous London house and appeared to many that whatever Barings undertook it was always very profitable.

However, by over self confidence, investing far too heavily in South America and being given wrong information about investments in Argentina the stage was set for a financial crisis. It was precipitated by the Buenos Aires Water Supply and Drainage Company's mismanagement against a background of political intrigue resulting in Barings holding £21 million of worthless stock in 1890.

The crisis burst on the London financial market towards the end of 1890 and could have pulled down many other merchant houses had not a rescue package been put together by the Bank of England and other merchants banks. Edward Baring resigned and never recovered from this catastrophe dying in 1897. Barings were almost forced to cease trading in the early months of 1891.

It was through the strenuous efforts of his son John, who took over the running of the house, that the loans made to Barings were cleared by the late 1890s so bringing to an end this unfortunate blemish on its history.

In 1891 Membland and its land was valued at £150,000, the hall's contents £10,000, 37 Charles Street, London, at £75,000 and £50,000 for Revelstoke's furniture and pictures. Everything had to go. The contents of Membland were sold and the hall put up for sale in 1895 with 4,135 acres of land. There were no acceptable bidders. In 1897, however, outlying areas of the estate were sold, then other parts went under the hammer until the large sale of 1915. The hall passed through various owners until it was demolished in 1928 and its materials sold off so bringing to a sad end this once splendid family residence with all its attendant buildings in this corner of Devon. Fortunately most of the minor buildings survive as private dwellings and the locality still has an air of distinctiveness about it.

Arthur L. Clamp, 92 Radford Park Road, Plymouth, PL9 9DX. February, 2001.

SOUTH DEVON

Illustrated Particulars and Plans of

MEMBLAND HALL

SOUTH DEVON

One of the 'Most Beautiful Residential, Sporting and Agricultural Estates in England.

Including the Costly Contents of the Mansion

Excepting Only Pictures, Silver, Silver Plate, Linen, China, Ornaments, and Personal Effects

The Property, Extends to about

2,722 Acres

in a Ring Fence.

WITH VACANT POSSESSION AT LADY DAY, 1916.

To be Offered by Auction by

Messrs. KNIGHT, FRANK & RUTLEY

(as a whole or in Lots) at the Royal Hotel, Plymouth, on Wednesday, July 21st, 1915, commencing at 11 a.m., precisely

Solicitors:
Messrs. TURNBULL & TILLY,
West Hartlepool.

Local Agents:
Messrs.
SKARDON, SONS & HOSKING,
Princess Square, Plymouth.

Land Agent:
C. W. TILLY, Esq.,
Estate Office, Thorp Perrow,
Bedale, Yorks.

Auctioneers:
Messrs. KNIGHT, FRANK & RUTLEY,
20, Hanover Square, London, W.,
10, Mount Street, W. and
100, Princes Street, Edinburgh.

GENERAL REMARKS

(The Estate as a whole.)

1. Membland Hall and Estate, consisting of about 2,722 Acres in a ring fence, is recognised as one of the most beautiful and distinguished County Seats in the South of England, and was, during the ownership of the late Lord Revelstoke, a favourite resort of Royalty, His Majesty the King, His late Majesty King Edward VII, and the late Empress Frederick having been entertained there.

2. The Estate is situated in the Parishes of Revelstoke, Newton Ferrers and Holbeton, between the Rivers Yealm and Erme, and the Southern Boundary for some five miles is the English Channel. Plymouth is about ten miles distant, Ivybridge, eight miles, and the Market Town of Modbury, six miles. The Railway Stations of Steer Point and Yealmpton, on the Great Western Railway, are within three and four miles respectively.

3. The Mansion stands on an eminence, occupies a delightful and bracing position with Southern aspect and possesses every modern convenience and comfort; some idea of the beautiful views to be obtained therefrom is given in the photographs in these particulars.

4. The Private Drives through the Estate are the most delightful in the Kingdom, the circular Marine Drive of some nine miles, principally along the rugged coast of the English Channel, and Westwards by the side of the River Yealm, forms a unique feature. From this drive distant glimpses of Cawsand Bay with the Cornish coast line beyond, Bryn Tor, the rocky island of Mewstone, Eddystone Lighthouse, and many well-known points on Dartmoor, are clearly discernable.

5. The property presents exceptional sporting advantages, possessing as it does, well-placed Woods and Plantations, affording excellent cover for the rearing of a large head of game. The formation of the Woods ensures birds flying high.

Hunting with the Dartmoor Foxhounds, Dartmoor Otter Hounds, Modbury Harriers and other Packs.

Sea and River Fishing.

Yacht Anchorage in the River Yealm, which at this point enters the sea and forms a safe Harbour.

The drawing room filled with many vases of flowers.

Extracts from the history of Baring Brothers Bank, London

In 1858 Baring Brothers were the London agents for the governments of Russia, Norway, Austria, the United States, Chile, Buenos Aires, New Granada, Canada, Nova Scotia, New Brunswick and Australia. They had 1,200 correspondents in different parts of the world; they had the personal accounts of the French Emperor and King Leopold of Belgium.

Thomas Baring in 1854 constantly met members of the government in the House of Commons, private houses and the clubs. Often his relations were among them. He was accepted by them as a member of the establishment whose discretion could be relied on and whose opinion on many issues was worth eliciting. He, for his part, made it his business to know the main lines of British policy.

For the next fifty years from the death of Thomas Baring in 1873 Baring Brothers house was dominated by father and son, Edward and John Baring, 1st and 2nd Barons Revelstoke. The two men were in many ways similar. Both were intelligent and cultivated, self confident to the point of arrogance. They were dignified in manner and imposing in appearance, men accustomed to and demanding the deference of the their inferiors. They were generous and public spirited, not over endowed with a sense of humour but felt by most people to be good company.

In 1886 six million pounds' worth of stocks and shares were handled by Barings for the flotation of the Guinness company, the family retaining £800,000 worth. Applications for the remaining £5.2 million were invited for Saturday, 23rd October and extra policemen were called in to be on hand in case the demands proved unusually heavy. Nothing prepared Barings for the frenzied tumult that took place. Baring's place was literally besieged. Policemen held back the pushing crowds of clerks, agents, messengers and city men and pains were taken to have one of the swing doors partly open to allow stock exchange men in. Some resourceful applicants wrapped their forms around stones and flung them through the windows.

The increase of business in 1873 led to demands for extra staff, the number of clerks continued to grow and the first woman joined the house in this year. Within a decade there were ten of them who had to be provided with a special entrance to the building with their own amenities so to protect them from male colleagues.

MEMBLAND HALL

with about

505a. 3r. 4p.

Situated in the Parishes of Holbeton and Newton Ferrers.

THE MANSION is approached by long Carriage Drives guarded by Entrance Lodges and terminating with a bold sweep at the Hall. One from the West leading off the Plymouth Road being about ½ mile in length and guarded by the

Picturesque Western Lodge

The other from the South Eastern or Coast side and is protected by the

Eastern Lodge

THE RESIDENCE affords every accommodation for a large establishment. It is entered from the carriage sweep through a

Massive Portico leading into the Outer Hall

Paved diagonally with Black and White Marble. On the right of this apartment is a

Commodious Cloak Room with Lavatories beyond

The Outer Hall opens into the

Grand Inner Hall or Saloon

40 ft. by 26 ft., and 25 ft. high.

This apartment is sub divided by Massive Pillars and Balustrade of Devonshire Marble, and has Marble Mantelpiece to match. It is decorated with Moulded Plaster Ceiling and Cornice, together with Panelled Walls finished White and lighted by a Large Bay Window.

6. The Accommodation of the Mansion (which is fitted with every comfort, particular attention having been paid to the Lighting, Drainage and Water Supply) can be summarized as follows:—

Reception Rooms:—Reception and Lounge Halls, Drawing Room, Billiard Room, Study, Dining Room, Morning Room and Boudoir.

Bed Room Accommodation.—Nineteen Principal Bed and Dressing Rooms, including two Suites, one including a Bed Room, Boudoir, Combined Dressing and Bath Room, the other a Bed, Dressing and Bath Room. There are also Nine Maidservants' Rooms, Seven Menservants' Rooms, Six Bath Rooms.

Complete Domestic Offices and Extensive Dry Cellarage.

Stabling for twenty-nine Horses, Coach-Houses, Coachmen's and Men's Rooms.

7. The Agricultural Portion of the Estate is situated in a thriving agricultural district, and within easy reach of good markets, and divided into well-appointed Farms of convenient size, with substantial and picturesque Homesteads. The Tenants are substantial and industrious, and the Rents are low. The Tenancies are chiefly yearly, expiring at Lady-day, 1916.

8. The Land is undulating, varying from 50 feet to 350 feet in elevation above the sea. The soil is light and fertile.

There are numerous picturesque Cottages and productive Small Holdings and Two Licensed Premises.

9. The Manor or reputed Manor of Noss Mayo, including the Right to Wreckage within the boundaries of the Manor, is the property of the Vendor, and will be included in the sale.

10. Possession of the Estate will be given at Lady-day, 1916, and by arrangement, with the exception of Battery Cottage and the Rifle Range, completion can be deferred until Michaelmas, 1916.

Markets and Market Days.

PLYMOUTH	10 miles	every Thursday and Saturday.
PLYMPTON	9 miles	1st Monday in the month.
MODBURY	6 miles	2nd " " "
IVYBRIDGE	8 miles	3rd " " "
YEALMPTON	3¼ miles	4th " " "

The entrance hall with palms and marbled columns.

Extracts from the history of Baring Brothers Bank, London

Three months later in 1873 Barings took a step that seemed relatively unimportant at the time but was to have most dire consequences. It sent as its agent to Buenos Aires, Nicholas Bouwer, a clerk of Dutch extraction, who had been employed by Barings for thirteen years. His terms of reference were to look out for suitable mercantile operations, and to pay attention to the Buenos Aires Drainage and Waterworks scheme which had received a loan in the same year. Bouwer introduced Barings to the trading house of Hales in Argentina whose principal partner was a Mr. Pearson, described as *a little too easy in business.*

In 1888 it was reported that the President of Argentina was a weak man who allowed the railway building mania to get out of hand and ran up debts out of all proportions to the immediately realizable assets of the country. A year later even Revelstoke was showing alarm. Our money market is getting tighter daily and with the great expansion of trade and continuous outflow of gold there will be a pinch for money towards the end of the year. Argentine securities of all kinds are depressed.

John Baring wrote from Buenos Aires in 1889 that if only its rulers would behave decently then the value of its stock would soar high. There is no limit to the riches of the republic. The bribery and corruption is quite awful, he told his father upon this return to London. After gleaning the principles of business in the offices of No. 8 Bishopgate, London, I am perfectly aghast as what goes on in the republic.

In 1890 the *New York Times* said that this catastrophe was like no other banking catastrophe; Barings were the greatest banking house of all the world whose signature has stood always and everywhere for an absolute guarantee.

From Paris it was written in 1891 that by saving Barings from this catastrophe the English banks are serving their own interests for, at this moment, the house of Barings is the keystone of English commercial credit and its collapse would provoke terrible consequences for the English trade in all parts of the world.

Acknowledgements

A brief remark made two years ago about Membland Hall and its very large estate led me into researching its story in booklet form with illustrations as a local record of the few years when it was the home of the large Baring family and to which many famous people visited it especially during the annual sporting and Christmas seasons. I wish to record my many thanks to various people who supported me in this pursuit. The staffs of the West Devon Record Office, the Plymouth and Exeter libraries, the archivists at Ing Barings office and the R.I.B.A. Library Photographic collection, both in London, and Revelstoke Museum, British Columbia, Canada. Also to L. Williams, M. Ellis and Mrs. M. Clooke and others who patiently listened and responded to my enquiries.

The Private Study

Decorated with Panelled Dado and Hand-painted Walls. Conveniently arranged in a recess is a bath, together with Water Closet. Adjoining is the

Morning Room

Having 3 ft. White Painted Dado and Marble Chimney-piece and Hearth, the Walls being lined with Silk. At the end of the Corridor is the

Billiard Room

23 ft. 6 in. by 22 ft. 6 in.,

With Glazed Doors opening on to the Garden Terrace.

The Principal Staircase

Rises from the Saloon to a Balcony which gives access to the Principal Bed Chambers and other apartments conveniently arranged

A Suite of

Principal Bed Room with bay window, with 4 ft. painted dado, surmounted by silk hangings and ornamental plaster ceiling; Boudoir, with bay window and oak parquet floor; communicating with a well-fitted Bath Room, the walls being faced with a White Dado, above which are hand-painted tiles, W.C. adjoining.

Another Suite

Includes a Large Double Bed Room, Louis XV. Sitting Room, combined Dressing and Bath Room, and W.C.

There is also a Double Bed Room, known as the "Yellow Room," with W.C. adjoining.

Fitted Organ by HELE & Co.,

Worked by Hydraulic Power, and having Two Manuals, with Five Stops to the Great Organ, Eleven to the Swell, and Three to the Pedals, together with Four Couplers. The Keyboard is enclosed by Panelled Mahogany Folding Doors. A side door leads from the Saloon to

The Garden Porch

communicating with the Terrace and Pleasure Grounds beyond. The Outer Hall, the Saloons and the Corridors on each floor are Heated by Hot-water Coils.

Approached from the Saloon on the right is an

Elegant Drawing Room

32 ft. by 19 ft. 6 in., and 13 ft. high.

From the windows of this room Most Delightful Views are obtained. The apartment is Decorated in Gold and White, with 4 ft. Panelled Dado and Panelled Walls with Raised Festooned Decorations and Dentil Cornice; the Ceilings being also divided into Ribbed Panels in relievo, with finely executed Central Paintings of Female Figures.

Grand Piano by BECHSTEIN.

To the left of the Saloon is the

Dining Room

37 ft. by 17 ft.

Having South aspect, with Folding Doors opening on to the Garden Terrace, Polished Oak Floor, Oak Overmantel, Massive Marble Chimney-piece, Kerb and Hearth and Tiled Cheeks.

A Serving Lobby

With Hot-plate is fitted for communication with the Corridor leading to the Domestic Offices. On the left of the Saloon the Corridor leads to

The dining room ready to receive guests for the evening meal.

Extracts from the history of Baring Brothers Bank, London

Until the middle of October, 1980, there were not half a dozen people in London who suspected that Barings were under serious pressure. Plenty of people were uneasy about what was going on. Within the house of Barings T. C. Baring had been predicting disaster in Argentina for several years.

Lord Revelstoke resigned from the management on 22nd November, 1890, he was broken hearted about the affair but accepted the fact changes would have to be made to Barings and that he would have no control on its future activities.

On 25th November, 1890, a circular letter announced that Baring Brothers and Company had transferred their business to a new company with limited liability to be called Baring Brothers and Co., Limited. The paid up capital was said to be a million pounds. John Baring, his son, will eventually head up this new company.

One thing is certain, it was observed in late 1891, their honor and honesty. Their character stands as high today as ever it did and this of itself will prove as good to them as an extra million of capital. It was this sympathy that was John Baring's greatest asset when he came to establish the new house.

Revelstoke, who had been the highest, had the furthest to fall. His entitlement to the largest share of the profits now made him responsible for a similar proportion of the losses. There was no question that Membland and the house in Charles Street, London, had to go with all the furniture and pictures.

1891: Membland, with 4,500 acres, was valued at £150,000 with a further £10,000 for the contents; 37 Charles Street, London, at £75,000 with £50,000 for Revelstoke's splendid French furniture and pictures. The work of stripping the houses of their rich contents began at once. When his son Maurice went back to Membland he remarked that everything had changed. There was no Christmas party and the household was going through a process of gradual reduction, the French governess was leaving, the stables were empty and the old glory of Membland had gone for ever.

1893: We consider Lord Revelstoke's house in London quite unique being freehold in the first place and having been almost rebuilt and then arranged and decorated in a style that is not equaled in any London mansion and having all the modern appliances such as electric lighting from its own dynamos, hydraulic lifts, etc. The house was still unsold when Revelstoke died in 1897.

A Double Bed Room known as the "Blue Room" with W.C. adjoining; a Double Bed Room, called the "Green Room," with Single Bed Room adjoining; together with a large fitted Bath Room, used as a Dressing Room, with W.C. An additional Water Closet and Housemaid's Cupboard.

The Second Floor provides the following accommodation :—Single Bed Room, Two Maid-servants' Rooms, Housemaid's Closet, Large Day Nursery, Single Bed Room, Wardrobe Room, Two other Single Bed Rooms, with commodious Box Room over, Bath Room, Water Closet and Housemaid's Closet. On the half-landing (approached by a separate passage) are Two Bachelors' Bed Rooms.

In the Tower are Double Bed Room and Water Closet on the First Floor; School Room on Third Floor; a Double Bed Room on the Upper Floor. There are also Two other good Bed Rooms.

The Servants' Bed Rooms

Are planned over the Domestic Offices, and approached by Separate Staircases. The Maidservants' Rooms consist of Two Double and Three Single Bed Rooms, Housekeeper's Bed Room, Bath Room, Water Closet, Housemaid's Closet and fitted Linen Room; there are also a Blanket Room and Housemaid's Sitting Room. The Menservants' Rooms, arranged over another portion of the Offices, comprise a Large Bed Room for Butler, Five Single Rooms, Bath Room and W.C.

The Domestic Offices

Which are completely shut off from the Reception Rooms, are commodious and suitably planned. They comprise Housekeeper's Room, fitted with cupboards and small lavatory, Store Room adjoining, Servants' Hall with panelled wall and open fire-place, Brushing Room, Drying Closet, Small Pantry, Lamp Room, Boot Room, well-lighted Kitchen, partly tiled and fitted with substantial modern range; Cook's Sitting Room and Store Room, Tiled Scullery, fitted with range, oven, three sinks and racks; Meat and Pastry Larders, Still Room, fitted with double oven and range of cupboards; Bake-house, fitted with large brick oven and sink; well-fitted China Room.

In the Basement is Ample Cellar Accommodation; Decanting Room, Butler's Room fitted with cupboards, Butler's Pantry with Strong Room, Store Room and Two Bed Rooms for Menservants.

The Outbuildings

are conveniently situated near the Mansion, and consist of Boothouse, Wood and Coal-houses, Box Room, well-fitted Gun Room, Carpenter's Shop, Cider Cellar, Oil House, and an excellent octagonal Game Larder fitted for hanging 2,000 head of Game.

The Steam Laundry

Admirably designed and fitted with Messrs. Bradford and Co.'s most approved appliances, and surrounded by extensive Drying Grounds.

Five-Roomed Cottage

Receiving and Packing Room, Washing House, Steam Drying Room, Ironing Room, Boiler and Engine House, Coal Store, Ash House and Water Closet.

The Electric Light

Is installed throughout the house, the supply being generated by a powerful and complete Plant, consisting of a 26-h.p. Hornsby-Ackroyd Oil Engine, with dynamo and batteries, all arranged in a set of modern buildings especially designed for that purpose. There are also adjacent is a

Private Gas Works

Situated about a quarter of a mile from the Mansion, consisting of Five Retorts, Purifier, Meter House, Coal House and Two Holders. This Plant has not been used by present owner, but the buildings connected with the works are all of modern design and construction;

Stone and Slated Cottage

for Engineer.

The Hall is fitted throughout with Electric Bells, and communication is also afforded between different apartments by Speaking Tubes. Electric Alarm Bells are fitted in case of fire.

9

Part of the corridor opening to the right to the entrance hall.

Extracts from the history of Baring Brothers Bank, London

John Baring, 2nd Lord Revelstoke after his father's death in 1897, was as autocratic as his father and in time almost vain but enjoyed better judgement and a capacity for calculation. If there had been no Baring crisis he might have inherited his father's recklessness as well, but he learned prudence the hard way and was never to forget it.

In 1910 out of a total of about £15.5 million in business just over half emanated from America. Three hundred and fifty credits were issued in New York in 1906. Among the transactions Barings financed were the import of shellac from India, hides from Hamburg, lemons from Italy, slippers from Turkey, skins from Russia, coffee from Brazil and silk from Japan.

In 1912 Barings remained a good place to work. Most of the staff remained loyal. Mr. John Warry, an employee, was hardly typical. On the 15th May Barings wrote to him stating you will have completed sixty years of service with the firm and we understand that, being in your 85th year of age, you would be glad to be relieved of your duties. He retired in June receiving full pay for the rest of the year and then a pension of £250 a year until his death.

In 1912 women were by now taken for granted to work at any levels except the most highest and lowest in Barings. They were mainly employed in the travellers letters department or the coupon department. As they had to frequently pass through the public parts of the office black dresses had to be worn with no objection to white collars and cuffs added to the dress. No coloured trimming or fancy blouses were to be worn during hours of business.

Plymouth Street Name
Many of the streets at Greenbank were laid out in the 1880s and 1890s at the time of the height of Membland Hall. This one commemorates the Barings of that period.

The Pleasure Grounds & Gardens

Are of a diversified character and their charms are enhanced by the gently undulating nature of the surface as well as by the natural beauty and maturity of their varied surroundings. On the southern side of the Mansion the Lawns are planned in terraces intersected by winding gravel paths; a broad Terrace flanks one side of the Mansion, overlooking a beautiful timbered Park which falls away to the valley on the Southwest to the mouth of the River Yealm. Grass Tennis Court with Rustic Summer-houses, and a Bowling Green. On the Eastern side of the Mansion is a Covered and Well-ventilated Tennis Court, built of stone and slated, with cement floor; and fitted with balcony at either end, and Dressing Room with Lavatory. There is a Private Cricket Ground with Ornamental Pavilion near the Tennis Courts from which extensive views of the Dartmoor range of hills are obtained. The Productive Kitchen Gardens consist of Two capital Walled Fruit and Vegetable Gardens sloping to the South, while adjoining the Laundry is a supplementary Kitchen Garden, the whole being well stocked in a thriving state. There are extensive

Well-heated Glass-houses,

Comprising Orchard House, 173 ft. long; Four Green Houses, together some 290 ft. in length; Two 4-division Vineries, Fern House, and Two Ranges of Hot Pits. The Contents of the Glass Houses will be included in the Sale.

Adjacent to the Garden is an

Agent's or Head Gardener's House,

Also another Six-roomed Cottage. Annexed to one of the garden walls is an extensive Range of Buildings forming Bothy, Potting Sheds and Fruit Store.

Ornamental Tea House on the Beacon Hill.

A Portion of this Lot extending to about 100 acres is at present let to Mr. B. Cane with Preston Farm, and the apportioned rent will be per £150 annum.

There are about 164 acres of this Lot at present let to Mr. R. B. Meathrel with Caulston Farm (Lot 6), and the apportioned rental will be per £182 annum.

Two Reservoirs

Of 54,000 and 40,000 gallons capacity respectively, for the storage of water rising from a powerful spring on the Estate, and whence it is carried through pipes by gravitation to capacious tanks in the upper part of house. An Independent Supply has also been provided for temporary use during repairs to main service, also for use of Steam Laundry. The Rain Water is collected in tanks on the roof, and provision has also been made for underground storage. Hydrants connected with the main water supply have been fixed on each side of the House for use in case of fire. The complete and modern system of

Drainage

With proper inspection chambers, traps and ventilators serves all parts of the Mansion and Outbuildings. The Drains discharge into a cesspool some distance from the house with overflow beyond.

The Stabling

Which is situated to the West of the Mansion, is divided into two distinct establishments, one forming

The Hunting Stables

Fitted with Musgrave fittings, built of stone with brick dressings and slated roof, arranged round a spacious yard, comprise Ten Loose Boxes, Hospital Box, covered Washing Yard, Shoeing Shop with Forge, Two Forage Stores, Coach-house, Saddle Room with Groom's Room over, etc.

The Household Stables

Fitted with the St. Pancras Ironworks Company's fittings, are also built of stone with brick dressings, and are conveniently planned round a large paved yard. They comprise Sixteen Stalls, Three Loose Boxes, Washing Box, Cleaning Room, Two Harness Rooms, large Double Coach-house, and covered Washing Yard; also accommodation for Six Helpers, Mess Room, and Suite of Six Rooms for Coachman, together with extensive Lofts. Electric Light is fitted throughout, and there is also a Turret Clock Tower.

The expansive gardens and greenhouse in front of the agent's house.

Vegetable and Fruit Gardens at Membland

The above photograph gives some idea of the extensive gardens that were laid out to serve the needs of the Baring family, their staff and the many visitors who came here mainly during the hunting and christmas seasons. The numerous heated greenhouses enabled the growing of many kinds of fruit and flowers for most of the year planned by the head gardener on duty in the gardening office with various staff working the land.

The inventory book of March, 1900, records the following details: Gardening office fitted with a pine writing desk with sixteen drawers, office stool, American stove and flue pipes, coils of hot water pipes and a 7 runged ladder. Packing shed. Potting shed. Mushroom shed. Furnace house. Harness room. Break house. Range of three peach houses. Orchard span roof greenhouse, about 173 ft. Four lean to frames. Range of four vinearies. Rosary. *Upper gardens:* Carnation house. Strawberry house. Range of four cucumber houses. Two ranges of hot pits. Fern house. Ninety pheasant rearing coops at Stoke Barn. Saw mill and a carpenter's shop.

No details of the wide range of vegetables grown were given. Occupants listed in 1891 living in the gardener's cottage were George Baker, 59 years, gardener, Mary A., wife, 61 years and Elizabeth, daughter, 29 years, no occupation.

THE SPORTING

The scale of the activities of the shooting season on the Membland estate can be seen by the following figures taken from the 1895 sale catalogue. Many friends of the Barings came down from London for the *sporting* and to enjoy the hospitality of Lord and Lady Revelstoke during the early autumn.

	1888/89	1889/90	1890/91	
Pheasants	2,769	4,111	4,630	Shot
Partridges	210	256	55	,,
Hares	185	238	151	,,
Woodcock	9	15	49	,,
Rabbits	746	630	126	,,
Various	33	73	63	,,

1,500 to 2,000 rabbits were killed annually chiefly on the Warren.

Two Stable Blocks
Twenty nine horses were kept at Membland Hall divided between *household* horses used for carriage work and *hunters* used during the annual hunting season. The upper view shows the entrance to the hunting stables with two Dutch gabled coach houses on either side. They were *fitted with Musgrave fittings around a spacious yard, 10 loose boxes, a hospital box, covered washing yard, shoeing shop with forge, bellows and blower tank, 2 forage stores, coach house, saddle room with groom's room over it.* (Italic taken from the 1900 inventory book.)

Household Stables
This view dates from about 1910, somewhat forlorn and unused since the crisis of 1891. They were *fitted with St. Pancras Ironworks Company's fittings, large paved yard, 16 stalls, 3 loose boxes, washing box, clearing room, 2 harness rooms, large double coach house and covered washing yard. Accommodation for 6 helpers, mess room, suite of 6 rooms for coachmen. Turret clock tower.* (Italic taken from the 1890's inventory book.)

Occupants of Coachman's Cottage and Stable Staff in 1891
William Bilkey, head aged 51 groom/coachman
Sarah Bilkey, wife aged 45
Mary E. Bilkey, daughter aged 21
Elizabeth A. Bilkey, daughter, aged 18
Florence T. Bilkey, daughter aged 14 scholar
Laura C. Bilkey, daughter aged 12 scholar
Willie Bilkey, son aged 6 scholar
Harold Bilkey, son aged 4
William Maker, aged 19 helper in stables
Sidney Hart, aged 18 helper in stables
John Dyer, aged 29 groom in stables
Harry P. Johnson, aged 19 groom in stables
Thomas Friend, aged 21 helper.
The Dutch styled gable building on the left is at the entrance to the household stables.

Membland Hall
A closer view of the south facing side of the mansion. The house was extended and remodelled in the late 1870s enhancing a much earlier building on this site to the tastes of Edward Baring following its purchase in 1877.

Cricket Pavilion
Family and guests watching a game of cricket at Membland Hall from the wooden pavilion which unfortunately no longer stands. However, the game would have provided a suitable afternoon's entertained for guests down from London for the weekend among the woodlands of the locality.

Membland Hall
A south facing view of the Mansion at its height sometime in the 1880s. It overlook terraces running down to extensive lawns providing a restful view over the nearby countryside.

1st Lord Revelstoke
This photograph of a painting by Rudolph Lehman shows Edward Baring on one of his many horses sometime in the 1880s. It depicts him at Membland Hall against an artist's background impression of part of the stable block.

1st Lord Revelstoke
He is seen here standing on the steps on the north side of Membland Hall again sometime in the 1880s. Note part of his crest on the wall behind and above the porch.

Membland Hall occupants listed in the 1891 census
Edward Lord Revelstoke, Head aged 62, merchant and banker.
Louisa E., Lady Revelstoke aged 51, wife.
Louisa Baring, Dame, daughter aged 20
Maurice Baring, son aged 16
Hugo Baring, son aged 14
Margaret Spencer, Dame, daughter aged 22 married
Christopher Spencer, son in law, aged 33 married
Robert T. Deacon, aged 43 butler/servant
Vincent C. Hodge, aged 19 footman/servant
Louisa Butat, male, aged 42 cook/servant
Frederick T. Evans, son aged 25 footman/servant
Louisa Tugday, aged 52 housekeeper
Jane Nimeslar, aged 27 house maid/servant
Blanche Tall, aged 19 house maid/servant
Mary Hawke, aged 22 house maid/servant
Selina Hogg, aged 22 kitchen maid/servant
Ellen Moore, aged 18 kitchen maid/servant
Charlotte Tarr, aged 29 ladies maid
Sarah Woods, aged 26 ladies maid
William Tracey, aged 18 valet/servant
Adele Butat, aged 32, visitor wife of cook

Steam Laundry

Erected in 1888 it was described as *admirably fitted with two of Bradford & Cos. washing and drying machines.* It had a receiving and packing room, washing house, steam drying room, ironing room fitted with an 18 ft. 6 ins. deal ironing bench, boiler and engine house, coal store, ash house and water closet. Mary Pepperell, aged 59, was the laundress in 1891, helped by her son William, aged 33, and Ann, daughter in law, aged 31 years.

Gas Manager's Cottage

Built in 1882 for the manager's family, it is short distance from the works and is now almost hidden to view from the road. John James was given as head of the family in 1891, his wife, Mary, was aged 44 years and their family was made up of three sons and one daughter, the three sons working at the gas works.

The initials stone of the gas works.

Estate Gas Works

Built in 1882 it consisted of five retorts, it had a purifying room, meter room and, nearby, two gas holders. Coal came up from Bridgend in a horse and cart. In 1891 John M. James, aged 47, was given as the gas manager assisted by his son, William, general labourer, John, another son, aged 14, fire stoker and Ernest as a carpenter.

Battisborough Cottages

This pair of cottages was built for two estate families a short distance from the estate blacksmith's forge and workshop now derelict in this hamlet on the eastern perimeter of Membland's land. They are dated 1884 and in 1891 Thomas E. Paige, blacksmith, aged 28, with his wife, Mary, also 28, with a son, Stanley, 6, and Hannah Bunker, mother in law, aged 70, were given as living in one of the cottages. The first occupants of the other cottages have not been identified from the records.

Covered Tennis Court

This was the largest room on the estate and was additionally used for the very large annual christmas party at which a play in French always took place. There was a balcony at each end for spectators. From the 1900 inventory book it is recorded that it was lit by gas jets from brass brackets with ground glass plates. The heating was from stoves *enclosed in perforated iron gratings with marble tops.*

Bull and Bear Lodge

Situated a mile west of Holbeton, this lodge with its imposing gates opened to a drive of three miles to Membland Hall presumbly for the convenience of members of the Bulteel family who lived in this area. It dates from 1889, a year before the financial crisis arose, and is known for its bull and bear statues on top of the gate columns signifying the union of the Baring and Bulteel families although these terms are well known in the stock market world used when the market is on the up *Bull market* and down *Bear market*.

Rowden Farm

Built in 1884 it comprised of 293 acres was then tenanted by William Wakeham who in 1891 was aged 45 years, his wife Sarah, 45 years, with one daughter, Alice, 2 years. William Mashford, Margaret Mashford and Jessie Brown, were listed as domestic servants. Farmer Wakeham was in occupation at the time of the 1915 sale of the Membland estate.

Eastern Lodge

This roundish building was erected in 1883 standing at the eastern entrance to the estate where the nine mile marine drive runs up from the coastline. The letters ECB are cut into the weather vane which, together with the building's distinctive architectural style, makes it stand out as yet another reminder of Edward Baring's ownership of this area of south west Devon.

Alston Farm

Built in 1890 and adorned with an ECB motif the rebuilding of the farms seems to have attracted young farmers to this area as Alston was worked by Henry Wilton, aged 39 years, in 1891, his wife, Margaret was 30 years, their son Harold, was 2 years, with Charles Pearce and Bessie Pallick given as a farm and domestic servant.

LADY BARING'S CARRIAGE WAY

This nine mile carriage way or marine drive, as it is sometimes called, was cut in the early 1880s to provide employment for local men and to enable Edward Baring's wife and children, sometimes with friends in a second carriage, to travel along this beautiful coastline.

It went from Membland mansion down to Bridgend, through Noss Mayo entering Passage Woods, alongside the estuary, on its way out to Mouthstone Point where it curved eastwards along the high cliffs towards Stoke, up to Beacon Hill where it curved north towards Eastern Lodge before descending down to Membland. It encompassed a large area of the Membland estate providing outstanding views towards Wembury and the sea and a refreshing morning or afternoon's carriage outing.

There were at least two tea houses along the route at which refreshments would be made available and a rest for the horses taken. One was at Warren Cottage and another at Beacon Hill, now a ruin, with a possible stop at Stoke House, maybe to walk down to the shore. Battery cottage, close to the Yealm estuary, although standing by the carriage way does not appear to have been a tea house, more a dwelling for an estate family when it was built.

There are very few references to this drive way except that a Mr. Yabsley was responsible for dynamiting the rocks to clear a way and then in the following winter it was widened to provide further employment to the team of men who had been working throughout the summer. It is now one of the most attractive walks in this area.

Battery Cottage

This takes its name from an early military battery which stood here guarding the entrance to the Yealm estuary. It stands alongside the nine mile marine drive on the headland but does not look as though it was used as one of the drive's tea rooms. Described as *a charming weekend residence* it was let to a Mrs. Reade in 1914 as a private dwelling with 341 acres of land.

Beacon Hill Tea House

This derelict small building stands on Beacon Hill about halfway between Stoke House and Eastern Lodge where the marine drive turns north on the final length of the carriage way. It does seem strange to have such a small building erected for this purpose but there are two references in the records that this was its purpose. Maybe it had other uses as well. The author is standing in the picture.

Warren Cottage

A familiar sight for hundreds of walkers nowadays along the coastal marine drive. Described as a large tea pavilion it was one of three along the nine mile drive affording rest and tea for the Barings and their friends and the carriage horses. Built in the 1880s it was occupied by Jessie Evans, 29 years old, gamekeeper, and his wife Elizabeth, 25 years old, in 1891.

Post Office Farm

This stands at Bridgend and takes its name from the time when it was used for a few years as a post office and telegraph office for receiving and despatching mail for the Membland estate as well as being a farm. It is easily recognised as an estate building and has the usual ECB initials embellished on its wall. Built in 1885 it was linked to the mansion by a private telephone line and in 1915 it was let to Mr. V. E. Irish together with 28 acres of farming land. The mail was collected and despatched twice a day originally to the railway station at Ivybridge for onward carriage to Barings Bank, London.

Extracts from the history of Baring Brothers Bank, London

Between 1865 and 1890 Barings were responsible for 28.7% of the North American railway stocks issued through London merchant banks worth £34.68 million. No other London competitor took more than 10% and yet like England's Indian empire, it largely came about through good fortune. The place in Canada where the east and west railroads met is called Revelstoke in British Columbia (see map).

It was written in 1848 that the interest of Barings be best served by wasting none of its resources on European business but turning its attention to the United States and the East. Business was booming there, confidence was high, the network of roads and railways spreading with astonishing speed. There was never a country so prosperous. The progress of everything in eight years is almost incredible, so wrote their representative.

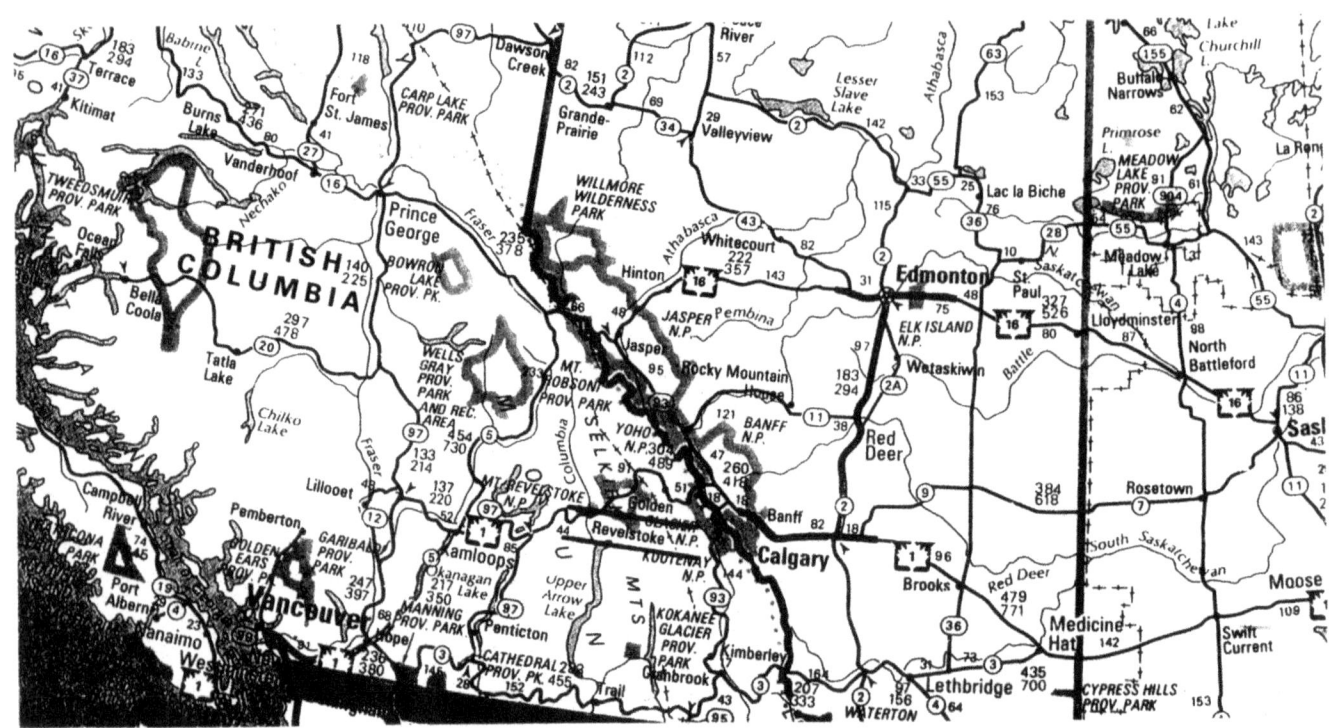

Revelstoke, British Columbia, Canada

The place at which the east and west railroads were joined on 7th November, 1885, is named *Revelstoke* in recognition of the huge financial investment made in the Canadian Pacific Railroad Co., by Baring Brothers Bank, London. They invested heavily in railroads across North America. The above map shows the location of the town and Revelstoke National Park.

150 ton Schooner Yacht "Waterwitch" on the Yealm estuary
This magnificent vessel was one of the pride and joys of Edward Baring who sailed it at Cowes regatta week each year and then sailed it down to Membland Hall mooring it in the Pool at Newton Ferrers as seen here. It was far too large to be moored at Kiln Quay. Two masted, coal fired, steam driven, it would be converted to sailing on the open seas. It is recorded that a captain Goomes followed by captain Bletchington were in charge of the vessel at various times.

Yealm Estuary
This view down part of the estuary shows the double doors of Kiln Quay boat house through which Lord Revelstoke's small boats entered the building mainly for winter mooring.

Kiln Quay Boat House
This large and prestigious water-front building at Newton Ferrers was built in 1884 to hold the small boats used by the Barings for travelling to and from Plymouth. The boats came in the on high tide and could safely be berthed in the lower part of the building along its full length under the first floor accommodation. In the 1895 sale catalogue it is described *as a yacht house, boat house and workshop with a large store and sail room with a five roomed cottage above.* Later described as a *boat house with living accommodation as well as winter shelter for the steam launches.*

Membland Hall
Two views of the mansion probably taken towards the end of the 1880s when the resplendent house was at its best. In a Devon directory of the same decade it records that Membland Hall was formerly the seat of Robert Roberts, Esq., subsequently belonged to J. D. Lewis, Esq., and is now the residential property of Edward Charles Baring, Esq., who erected there a mansion.

St. Peters Church, Revelstoke

Situated overlooking the Noss Mayo creek it was built in the years 1880-81 at the expense of the 1st Lord Revelstoke. Costing £35,000 it was designed by J. P. St. Aubyn and constructed under the watchful eye of the clerk of works, G. W. Crosbie, who implemented his Lordship's ideas on design evident throughout the interior. There is a commemorative window to his wife and, next to it, himself. The family grave backs on to the outside of the altar wall. This church replaces the much older one at Stoke beach which had started to fall into a ruin and was a long way from the growing village of Noss Mayo. Its position was also quiet convenient to Membland Hall. It matches to some extent Newton Ferrers church high above the main creek and village. The funerals here of the 1st Lord Revelstoke in 1897 and his son, the 2nd Lord Revelstoke in 1929, were attended by many dignitaries and representatives from the London merchant banks. The newspaper reports about them are well worth reading.

Church Cottage

Erected in 1883 two years after the church was opened it had ground accommodation for two coaches, stables, a harness room and a small gas engine for generating lighting in St. Peters. The Barings came down from Membland Hall leaving their horses and one or coaches in this cottage. In 1891 William Clarke, aged 59, sexton, was living here with his family above the stables. Sarah, his wife, was 57 and Annie their daughter was 19. A godson, William Foster aged 5, was staying with them.

The Baring's grave at St. Peter's Church, Revelstoke

In loving memory of
Edward Charles 1st Lord Revelstoke
Born 13th April 1828 Died 17th July 1897
Who built this church
And of
Louisa Emily Charlotte his wife
Born 18th June 1839 Died 16th October 1892
This cross was erected by their children.

John
2nd Lord Revelstoke
Born 7th September 1863
Died 19th April 1929
He is buried with them.

It was written of John in the 1920s:
He had been on the Court of the
Bank of England since 1898,
Privy Councillor since 1903,
became Receiver General of the Duchy
of Cornwall in 1908, was King George V's
closest financial adviser, became Lord
Lieutenant of Middlesex in 1926.
He was the indispensable man of
British financial life. He did not marry.

19th April, 1929, Death of 2nd Lord
Revelstoke.
Unsettled estate of £2,429,000 of which
duty of £1,087,000 was paid in death duty.

Newspaper article of 23rd July, 1897.

Arthur L. Clamp – the man behind the books

Arthur Leslie Clamp was a man of boundless energy with a passion for helping others, particularly through his love of history. A printer by trade, he started his career in a printing company before moving his family from Exeter to Plymouth to teach at the Plymouth College of Art and Design, where he eventually became the Head of the Printing Department.

Arthur with his five children.

A Devoted Family Man

Despite his love of teaching, Arthur prioritised his family, always making it home by 5:30pm for tea. He and his wife, Rosemary, raised five children: Susan, Angela, Elizabeth, David, and Steven. Arthur would often combine his love of family and history by taking his children on Sunday walks, encouraging them to appreciate historical monuments by taking photos or making crayon rubbings of gravestones for his books. The family home at 203 Elburton Road was a hub of activity, with a large garden, featuring a two-storey fort and a makeshift swimming pool.

A Lifelong Learner and Adventurer

Arthur's thirst for knowledge extended beyond history to a deep curiosity about the world. He was passionate about exploring different cultures, traditions, and cuisines, often taking advantage of his long summer holidays as a teacher to travel to places like India, Russia, South America, the middle east and the USA, sometimes bringing one of his children along. This adventurous spirit even influenced his home life, as seen by the short-lived family tradition of steam-cooking vegetables after a trip to Iceland.

History is a prominent feature of family days out

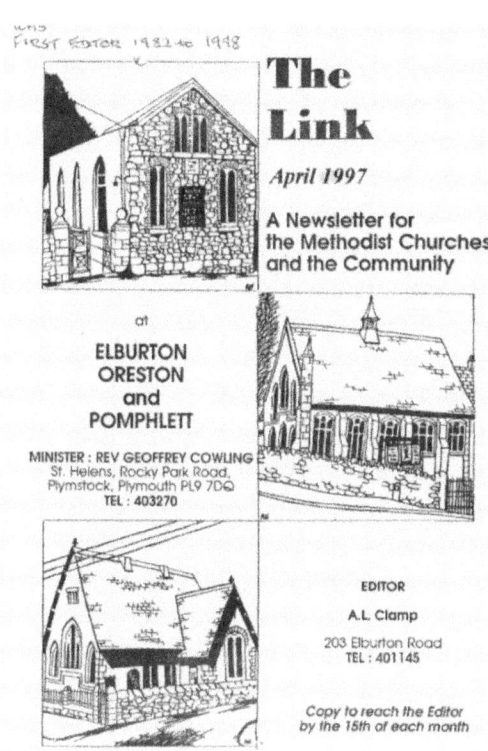

Community and Philanthropic Spirit

His commitment to serving others was evident in his long-standing involvement with the Elburton Methodist Church. He was the Sunday School Superintendent for over 15 years and served as the editor of the wider church's monthly newsletter, "The Link," for a similar duration. After Rosemary's very sad passing, Arthur later remarried and, following a chance encounter with a professor from India, established a connection with a missionary school in Chennai. Together with his new wife, Christine, he co-founded a "Sponsor a Child's Education" program that continues to this day.

*Pictured left – The cover of 'The Link' complete
with hand drawn sketches of each church by Angela
Below right – Arthur Clamp promoting his latest book
Below left – Arthur at home with his first wife, Rosemary
Below centre – Arthur on holiday with his second wife, Christine*

A Legacy of Learning and Positivity

Arthur's greatest passion was history, which he brought to life through tireless research, documentation, and the many books he authored. He was driven by a need to "never be stuck in a rut," constantly seeking new experiences, meeting new people, and expanding his knowledge. With a positive attitude and a great sense of humour, he was always ready to help others, leaving a lasting impact on his family and community. His children, Susan, Angela, Elizabeth, David, and Steven, remember him with love and gratitude.

David Clamp, 2025

A Legacy of Local History

Below is the story of how Arthur L Clamp began writing books, in his own words, drafted shortly before he passed away in 2001. I have only made minor alterations to this text, correcting grammatical errors that he did not survive to correct himself. When I first discovered this text, I was shocked to see my name mentioned. It seems that, unbeknownst to me, I shared my first PC with him. I suspect he used it during the day when I was at school, although I do have one memory of sitting with him and showing him how it worked. It has been a pleasure to pick up where he left off and see his books republished and redistributed, and to know that I was part of the story, even back then. It was also fascinating to discover that his pricing structure matches the way I have tried to price the books, with a third going to local sellers and the rest covering printing costs with a little left over for my expenses.

I am his eldest grandson, and it is a privilege to curate his legacy, which we are calling 'The Clamp Collection'. The very last line of the text originally reads "The following pages list all the titles." Sadly, that page is missing and we have no record of all the books he published and knowing that some of those were researched by other authors makes the process of finding them even harder. I look forward to one day completing the collection and seeing them all available again. And maybe, one day, I'll even start writing my own to add to the series. For now, here is his story in his own words.

Steven Gibson, 2025

Writing and Publishing Booklets on Local Topics and Areas

I started this interest in either 1968 or 1969 when living in Woodford. I had by these dates established the Department of Printing and I think I must have been looking for something different to do. The first titles were of A5 size proofed from type set at Clarke, Doble and Brendon, Ltd., Plymouth printers, and then made up into pages and printed at Sawtell and Neilson, Ltd., Totnes.

Then began a slow process of getting them out to shops, etc. which proved to be more time consuming and difficult than actually researching, writing and getting the books into print. However, I persisted and opened a business account with Barclays Bank on the Broadway. I was advised to give it a title so I called it "Westway Publications". There came along another problem, one of storage of paper and finished books which was solved when the family moved to Elburton in 1970.

I changed the printer to Penwell, Ltd., Callington, Cornwall, as he was then just setting up himself and his prices seemed very reasonable. I did not get any of the printers to make up the complete books. I hand folded the flat printed sheets, stitched the books on a small manual table stitcher and trimmed them in a small hand turned guillotine which I bought from someone in Penzance for £40. It was brought up in a van.

The trouble and time going to and fro to Callington was too much so I transferred the printing to PDS Printers, Prince Rock, Plymouth, and I have been with them ever since. Now they are at Plympton which is easy to reach and they fold the flat sheets which was turning out to be a long chore which only saved a small part of the printing costs.

All my first titles were written by myself. I took the photographs and developed them in the loft of the house, the type was set by now on a computer situated in the house at Elburton from which I had collected photographic lengths of text to cut up and law down as pages.

At some point I decided that I would do my own film processing of lith film so I bought a large second hand process camera from Kingsbridge and learnt through trial and error to make line negatives of the text and halftone negatives of the illustrations which proved more difficult than I anticipated. The main problem was trying to keep the developer in the large dish at the correct temperature as any change would affect the developing time. I replaced this old camera with a brand new one bought from Croydon, Surrey, costing £900. This has turned out to be a great asset cutting out an expensive part of the printer's costs and one crucial aspect of the work which I could control.

By the middle 1970s there were many outlets I had contacted in Plymouth, up to Dartmoor, Exeter, around to Torbay, Totnes, Dartmouth and the South Hams. The market for local books was much greater than I had first thought and through getting to know many local people undertaking research themselves had the chance to help and make up books for other people who had in most instances, got together a collection of photographs with some text in a rather muddled way. Through my experience in print I was able to shape up their work and get it into print and in every case I had to pay the printer and let the person have the royalties. In the majority of titles produced in this manner this was another way of producing titles and it did give some profit to my work. However, I must say that in a few cases I lost out by either the other person getting the numbers wrong, not returning any monies from stock I delivered or they thought that more of their books should have been sold.

The print run was usually 1,000 copies and from time to time I have had reprints of 250 copies. It took about ten years to clear the first print run so I always had large stocks in the garage, workshop, etc. The numbers sold during the early years was about 7,000 copies a year increasing to around 9,000 copies and for the whole of the enterprise about 500,000 have been sold. The booklets have become part of the local scene and many people collect them, shops regularly order copies and I go around certain areas month by month restocking or replacing titles as necessary.

During the past year or so I have started setting the text on a Packard Bell PC, something which I should have done some years back. I share it with Steven Gibson, my grandson. There appears to be no end to the market for local books, but I could not earn a regular income because of the long time it takes to sell stock.

However, now exceeding 100 titles made up mainly of A4 twenty-four page booklets, some folded guides, with selling prices set with a third going to the shop which is the trade custom, the original idea has been quite successful and could go on for ever.

Apart from monetary benefits, however spasmodically these might be, I have learnt a lot myself, met many interesting people and have become part of the local scene with requests to give talks and to advise people about getting into print.

Arthur L Clamp, 2001

This newspaper article, published by the Evening Herald on 17th August 2001, forms a good record of his life. Just as he encourages us to learn more about local history, we encourage you to learn a little about him. For that reason, we have included these pages at the back of all the most recently republished books, in honour of his memory and recognition of his contribution to the community.

www.ingramcontent.com/pod-product-compliance
Lightning Source LLC
Chambersburg PA
CBHW061408070526
44584CB00031B/4191